One time, after submitting a storyboard to Toriyama Sensei, he gave me this advice. He said, "What makes *Dragon Ball* so distinct and quirky is how it takes an ordinary concept or design and tweaks it ever so slightly."

Sensei... Isn't that the fundamental difference between a genius and a normal person...? Anyhow, I'm working hard to cross that divide!

—Toyotarou, 2018

Toyotarou

Toyotarou created the manga adaptation for the *Dragon Ball Z* anime's 2015 film, *Dragon Ball Z: Resurrection F*. He is also the author of the spin-off series *Dragon Ball Heroes: Victory Mission*, which debuted in *V-Jump* in Japan in November 2012.

Akira Toriyama

Renowned worldwide for his playful, innovative storytelling and humorous, distinctive art style, Akira Toriyama burst onto the manga scene in 1980 with the wildly popular *Dr. Slump*. His hit series *Dragon Ball* (published in the U.S. as *Dragon Ball* and *Dragon Ball Z*) ran from 1984 to 1995 in Shueisha's *Weekly Shonen Jump* magazine. He is also known for his design work on video games such as *Dragon Quest*, *Chrono Trigger*, *Tobal No. 1* and *Blue Dragon*. His recent manga works include *COWA!*, *Kajika*, *Sand Land*, *Neko Majin*, *Jaco the Galactic Patrolman* and a children's book, *Toccio the Angel*. He lives with his family in Japan.

SHONEN JUMP Manga Edition

STORY BY **Akira Toriyama**
ART BY **Toyotarou**

TRANSLATION **Toshikazu Aizawa, Christine Dashiell, and Caleb Cook**
LETTERING **Paolo Gattone and Chiara Antonelli**
TOUCH-UP ART **James Gaubatz**
DESIGN **Shawn Carrico**
EDITOR **Rae First**

DRAGON BALL SUPER © 2015 BY BIRD STUDIO, Toyotarou
All rights reserved. First published in Japan in 2015 by SHUEISHA Inc., Tokyo.
English translation rights arranged by SHUEISHA Inc.

The stories, characters and incidents mentioned
in this publication are entirely fictional.

Printed in Italy

Published by VIZ Media, LLC
P.O. Box 77010
San Francisco, CA 94107

10 9 8
First printing, May 2019
Eighth printing, May 2024

  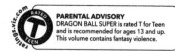

PARENTAL ADVISORY
DRAGON BALL SUPER is rated T for Teen
and is recommended for ages 13 and up.
This volume contains fantasy violence.

DRAGON BALL SUPER

THE DECISIVE BATTLE! FAREWELL, TRUNKS!

5

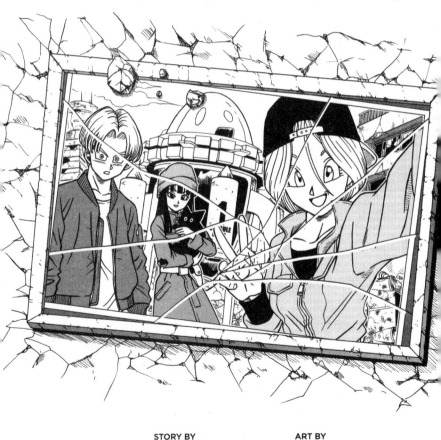

STORY BY
Akira Toriyama

ART BY
Toyotarou

CAST OF CHARACTERS

UNIVERSE 7

Beerus

Whis

Shin, Lord of Lords, Universe 7

Gowas, Lord of Lords, Universe 10

Son Goku

Vegeta

Trunks

Bulma

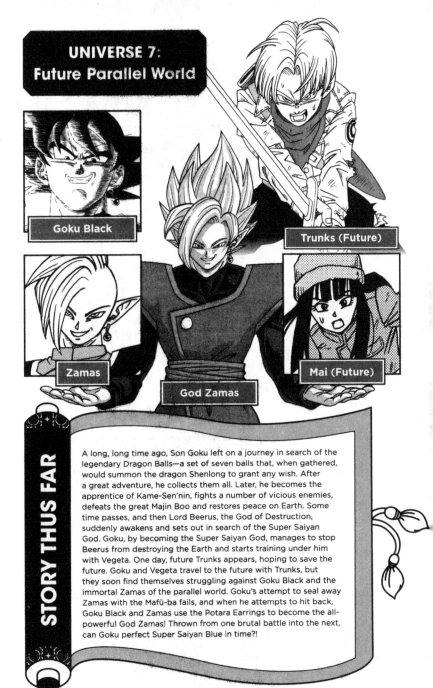

UNIVERSE 7: Future Parallel World

Goku Black

Trunks (Future)

Zamas

God Zamas

Mai (Future)

STORY THUS FAR

A long, long time ago, Son Goku left on a journey in search of the legendary Dragon Balls—a set of seven balls that, when gathered, would summon the dragon Shenlong to grant any wish. After a great adventure, he collects them all. Later, he becomes the apprentice of Kame-Sen'nin, fights a number of vicious enemies, defeats the great Majin Boo and restores peace on Earth. Some time passes, and then Lord Beerus, the God of Destruction, suddenly awakens and sets out in search of the Super Saiyan God. Goku, by becoming the Super Saiyan God, manages to stop Beerus from destroying the Earth and starts training under him with Vegeta. One day, future Trunks appears, hoping to save the future. Goku and Vegeta travel to the future with Trunks, but they soon find themselves struggling against Goku Black and the immortal Zamas of the parallel world. Goku's attempt to seal away Zamas with the Mafū-ba fails, and when he attempts to hit back, Goku Black and Zamas use the Potara Earrings to become the all-powerful God Zamas! Thrown from one brutal battle into the next, can Goku perfect Super Saiyan Blue in time?!

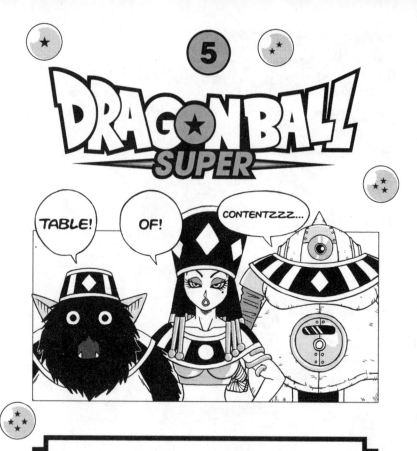

5

DRAGON BALL SUPER

CHAPTER 25: WILL IT BE GOKU?! OR ZAMAS?!

HAH!!

GAH!!

WOOSH

ZOON!

BAM

8

THUD

HAAAH!!

DAMMIT ...!!

VOON

GHHRRK

HAAH!

HAAH ...!

...IMMOR-TAL!

I AM...

RRRIP

BURBL
BURBL

HRAAH!!

KKRRKKK

...ANY DAM-AGE!

I WON'T TAKE...

AAAH...

!!

GAAH!

FWOOOSH

UGH!

THERE'S NO WAY...I'M LETTING YOU RECOVER NOW.

HUFF

BAM

ZSSHH

TCH... I DON'T HAVE MUCH TIME LEFT TO FIGHT LIKE THIS EITHER.

HUFF

HE'S LOSING THE ABILITY TO CONTROL THE BLUE POWER WITHIN HIM.

WHAT?! REALLY?!

KAKAROT'S BODY IS PROBABLY ALREADY NEARING ITS LIMIT.

G-GOKU'S NOT LOOKING SO GOOD.

...I'LL JUST HAVE TO TAKE MY CHANCES.

AT THIS POINT...

GHHKK ...

HUFF

HUFF

HUFF

HUFF

HUFF

HUFF

FWSH

...THAT TECHNIQUE MIGHT JUST TAKE HIM DOWN.

EVEN IF HE'S IMMORTAL...

THIS IS HIS LAST CHANCE.

THERE WON'T BE A NEXT TIME.

B-BUT IF HE DOES THAT--

HE'S PLANNING TO RELEASE HIS REMAINING POWER WITH HIS NEXT ATTACK.

HUH? THERE'S A BLUE AURA AROUND GOKU'S FIST!

...!

22

DESTRUC-
TION!!

EEK!!

MAI !!

BLOOP

YANK

WHAT'RE YOU DOING?!

Y... YOU...

FLINGG

ZOOSH

IT'S A SHAME THAT A GOD WHO STANDS AT THE APEX OF ALL CREATION SHOULD WIN IN SUCH A SHAMEFUL WAY...!

ZING

...TO NEVER BOTHER WITH MORTALS AGAIN.

ZAMAS!!!!

I'LL TAKE THIS AS A LESSON...

29

THIS PLANET IS A PAIN. I'M GOING TO WIPE IT OUT.

NOW THEN.

...CREATING THEM AGAIN.

OR RATHER...

IT'S... IT'S OVER.

AH... AH...

AH... AH...

THADUMP

!

...

AH...

GAH... AH...

...!

TH-THIS MUST BE—

AN HOUR'S PASSED SINCE ZAMAS FUSED!!

IT'S BEEN AN HOUR.

GNOOOOOOO

?

...

GHHHH...

GHHHRKK...

OVER THE PAST HOUR, THEY MAY HAVE JOINED ON A CELLULAR LEVEL.

THOUGH WE CALL IT A FUSION, THEY'RE BOTH ZAMAS.

WHAT?!

THEY'RE REJECT-ING...

...THE CANCEL-LATION?!

BOTH ZAMASES ARE RE-JECTING THE SPLIT.

B-BUT THEY'RE SPLITTING DIFFER-ENTLY THAN GOKU AND VEGETA.

WE ARE ONE...!

ONE GOD IS PLENTY ENOUGH.

GWOOO

I THOUGHT TIME WAS UP!

W-WHAT'S GOING ON?

I AM...THE ONE AND ONLY GOD.

MAI!

GAAH!!!

BOOSH

THUD

!!

HUH?!

YOU...!

WHA—

...NOT SUP- POSED TO BE IMMOR- TAL...

YOU'RE...

KLTR

ZLSH

SNAP

GRAB

39

GLORP

WHAT?!

W-WHY DO YOU LOOK LIKE THAT?!

42

D-DAMMIT. THEY'RE BOTH EQUALLY STRONG.

HA HA HA...

WHAT'S GOING ON HERE?!

TH-THIS COULDN'T GET ANY WORSE...

N-NOW THERE ARE TWO GOD ZAMASES!

SMAK

BASH

HE'LL ALWAYS REVIVE HIMSELF.

IT'S NO USE, VEGETA.

TW CH

TW CH

ZAMAS IS DISMEMBERED.

BLRP.

BLRP.

BLRP.

BLRP.

WRIGL

WRIGL

YOU COULD'VE GOTTEN YOURSELF KILLED, DAD!!

LAUNCHING A TECHNIQUE LIKE THAT WITH YOUR CURRENT STRENGTH...

HJFF

HJFF

FWP

FWP

WE CAN'T LEAVE ZAMAS LIKE THIS.

WHAT DO YOU MEAN RUN AWAY?

...

VEGE-TA! GOKU!

THIS IS OUR CHANCE TO RUN AWAY!

ZWOOOSH

H-HOLD ON A SECOND!

HUH?!

51

CHAPTER 26: THE DECISIVE BATTLE! FAREWELL, TRUNKS!

UGH...

UH...

VEGETA, TAKE MY HAND!!

TCH...

VWEEEN

PARALLEL WORLDS ARE NOT THE ONLY THING WE'RE GOING TO DESTROY!

GOWAS AND I WILL HEAD BACK WITH THE RING OF TIME. EVERYONE ELSE, GET IN THE TIME MACHINE!

TMP

1 CAPSULE CORP.

BUT ZAMAS SAID HE'S GONNA DESTROY THE REST OF THE PARALLEL WORLDS TOO!!

WE HAVE NO OTHER CHOICE!

ARE WE SERIOUSLY LEAVING WITH HIM STILL ALIVE?!

...!

CAPSULE CORPORATION

WHO SAID WE'D USE THE RING OF TIME?

CHASE US?! THAT'S CRAZY! YOU CAN'T USE THE RING OF TIME TO TRAVEL TO THE PAST!

THAT JERK...

TH-THERE ARE A LOT MORE OF THEM NOW!

I WON'T STOP CHASING YOU NO MATTER WHERE YOU GO!

PAST OR NOT, GO AHEAD AND RUN WHEREVER YOU WANT!

"LONG AGO, THERE WAS A HUMAN CIVILIZATION IN UNIVERSE 12 THAT POSSESSED HIGHLY SOPHISTICATED TECHNOLOGY. THEY INVENTED A DEVICE THAT COULD SEND A PERSON BACK IN TIME."

DAMMIT...!

ZAMAS...TO THINK HE'D REMEMBER THAT!

!

WHAT DID HE SAY ?!!!

I HAVE A TIME MACHINE OF MY OWN!

THE ONE THAT WAS MADE IN UNIVERSE 12!

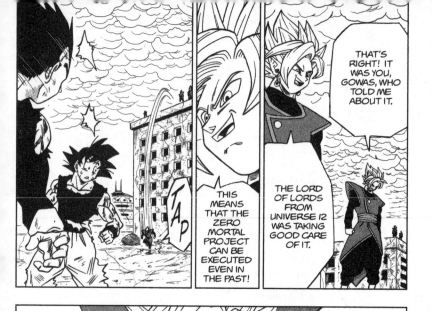

THAT'S RIGHT! IT WAS YOU, GOWAS, WHO TOLD ME ABOUT IT.

THE LORD OF LORDS FROM UNIVERSE 12 WAS TAKING GOOD CARE OF IT.

THIS MEANS THAT THE ZERO MORTAL PROJECT CAN BE EXECUTED EVEN IN THE PAST!

...AND TERMINATE MANKIND THERE!

AND TO START, I SHALL VISIT THE WORLD WHERE YOU ALL CAME FROM...

THAT IS...

BUT...

W-WHAT...?!

!!

DOES THAT MEAN, EVEN IF WE ESCAPE, HE'LL JUST COME AFTER US?!

HOLD ON...

...

YOU MUST GIVE UP AND LET YOURSELF BE KILLED BY MY HANDS.

THAT'S RIGHT...

KAKAROT!

FATHER!! GOKU!!!

W-WHAT ARE YOU SAYING?!!

THE REST OF YOU SHOULD GO BACK AND PRAY FOR A MIRACLE...

I'M STAYING HERE. I'LL FIGHT THEM OFF UNTIL THE END.

HMPH...

VEGETA...

...

IF YOU'RE STAYING, SO AM I.

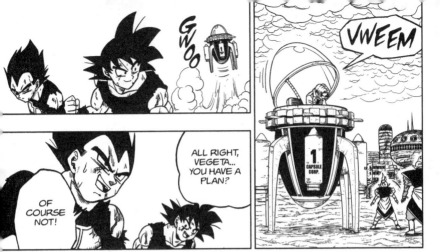

GWOO

VWEEM

ALL RIGHT, VEGETA... YOU HAVE A PLAN?

OF COURSE NOT!

THEN LET'S DO THIS TO-GETHER.

I SEE... THAT'S ALL.

GO WILD UNTIL YOU DIE.

HA!!!

HAA!!!

IF ONLY I HAD A SENZU BEAN WITH ME...

THIS IS FINE BY ME. AT LEAST I'LL GET TO SEE THE BIGGEST PAIN IN MY BUTT DIE...

I NEVER THOUGHT I'D MAKE MY LAST STAND LIKE THIS...

WISH I COULD GO CRAZY AS A SUPER SAIYAN, ESPECIALLY IN MY LAST BATTLE...

DARN... I DON'T HAVE AN OUNCE OF STRENGTH LEFT.

YOU SAID IT!

!

...

THIS IS...

HM?

I'M CERTAIN HE IS. NO ONE CAN DEFEAT THE LORD OF EVERYTHING.

HMM... THE LORD OF EVERYTHING?

IS THE LORD OF EVERYTHING IN THIS TIMELINE STILL AROUND?

HEY! KAIÔ-SHIN.

HUH?

TRUNKS! HOLD ON.

WHY ARE YOU ASKING ME NOW?

YOU THINK THIS THING WILL WORK ON THE LORD OF EVERYTHING HERE?

WE'RE ALL GOING BACK TOGETHER!!

THAT'S ...!

GOKU...

KLIK

WHAT'S HE SAYING ...?!

WHAT?

FWIP

WHAT ?!!!!

!!

PAT PAT

...!

...

THUD

...!

GAH!

THE L-LO...

TH-THAT IS...

THE LORD OF EVERY-THING ...!!!

MY NAME'S SON GOKU.

ARE YOU THE ONE WHO CALLED ME?

WHO ARE YOU?

I'M A FRIEND OF YOURS IN A DIFFERENT TIMELINE.

WHY IS THE LORD OF EVERY-THING HERE?!

W-WHY IS HE HERE?

...

HEY! ZENÔ-SAMA.

R-RUN
...!

W...

WORLD
?!!

A WORLD
LIKE THIS...

TSK...

LORDS OF LORDS! YOU MUST HURRY AND GO BACK TOO!!

Y-YES.

THIS IS BAD!! VEGETA! GET IN THE TIME MACHINE!!

FWIP

GO, TRUNKS!!!

GRP

GRP

VMMM

WSH

74

PSHHH
PSHHH

VMM

I FEEL SICK...

UGHHH...

...BACK...?

ARE WE...

IS EVERYTHING ALL RIGHT, GOKU...?!!

UH...

OH MY...

KERPLUNK

VRRR

TRUNKS AND EVERY- ONE ARE BACK!!

HUG

BMF

SHOOM!

BWOO

THANKS, KIBITO!

PHEW...

STILL... I WOULD SAY IT'S BETTER THAN LOSING EVERYTHING...

YES, THE LORD OF EVERYTHING DE-STROYED IT ALONG WITH ZAMAS...

AFTER ALL, TRUNKS'S FUTURE IS GONE FOREVER.

YES... I WONDER WHAT HAP-PENED TO US...

HEY, SHU... LOOKS LIKE MAI WAS THE ONLY ONE OF US LEFT IN THE FUTURE.

...

IT SEEMS YOU'RE DOING GREAT...

OH... YOU'VE GROWN UP...

SHU!

PILAF!

MAI, I MEAN THE BIG ONE!

HEY!

YOU SHOULD GREET HIM!

LORD BEERUS HAS ARRIVED.

HMM, THERE'S SOMETHING I WANT TO ASK YOU...

Y-YES, BUT...

YOU TOO, PILAF. YOU LOOK LIKE YOU'RE DOING WELL YOURSELF!

MAI!

IN THE FUTURE, ARE WE...

I BET YOUR POWER WASN'T GOOD ENOUGH TO DEFEAT HIM AFTER ALL.

HMPH...I CAN TELL YOU HAD A REALLY HARD TIME.

BEERUS! WE MANAGED TO DEFEAT ZAMAS!

HE IS THE GOD OF DESTRUCTION FROM UNIVERSE 7.

LORD BEERUS?

NOW, TELL ME EVERYTHING THAT HAPPENED.

HA HA HA...I KNEW YOU WOULD SAY THAT.

GAB GAB WAH WAH SIZZL

I GET IT. THEY ARE THE PERFECT MATCH...

SIGH ...

THANKS!

TRUNKS, YOU TRY THIS TOO!

YOU SHOULD TRY THAT.

RIGHT?

I CAN'T BELIEVE IT. THIS IS SO GOOD...

YOUR SINS MAKE ME SPEECH-LESS!

YOU EVEN MADE USE OF THE LORD OF EVERY-THING AT THE END...

YOU DAMN FOOL! YOU ALMOST GOT ME KILLED!

WHAT?! YOU WENT TO THE FUTURE TOO, KAIŌ-SHIN...?!

I FEEL SO STUPID... I'M DONE HERE.

YOU ALMOST GOT US KILLED TOO.

THOUGH I DIDN'T THINK HE'D DESTROY THE ENTIRE UNIVERSE.

THAT WAS THE ONLY THING I COULD THINK OF.

RIGHT... IN THE END, TRUNKS'S FUTURE IS GONE...

YES...

THAT'S WHAT I THOUGHT AT FIRST, BUT...

...

YOU'RE RIGHT. PERHAPS IT WAS GOOD SINCE YOU PUT THE PARALLEL WORLDS IN ORDER!

WELL, HAVING TOO MANY PARALLEL WORLDS IS NEVER A GOOD THING.

AND WE PROTECTED THE REST OF THE PARALLEL WORLDS-- IT WASN'T THE WORST OUTCOME.

STILL, WE MANAGED TO DEFEAT ZAMAS.

DIDN'T YOU SAY WE COULDN'T GO BACK THERE ANYWAY, RIGHT?

HUH?

DO YOU EVEN REALIZE THAT THESE TWO HAVE NO PLACE TO GO BACK TO ANYMORE?!

YOU'VE GOTTA BE KIDDING!!

I MANAGED TO BYPASS THE NEW PARALLEL CAPACITOR. WE ARE NOW ABLE TO TRAVEL TO ALL DIFFERENT KINDS OF FUTURES.

CHANGING FREQUENCIES IN THE TRANSPORTER CAN LET US JUMP INTO THE PARALLEL WORLDS.

MADAM, I WAS RIGHT!

SLIDE

I DIDN'T KNOW YOU WERE THIS SMART...

I STILL HAVE A LONG WAY TO GO...

YOU HEARD HIM...

WHAT FOR? YOU DON'T NEED THAT ANYMORE.

CAN YOU REFUEL THE TIME MACHINE FOR ME?

BULMA!

AH!

THESE JERKS... THEY JUST KEEP IGNORING THE RULES OF THE UNIVERSE!

LET'S JUST PRETEND WE DIDN'T SEE IT THIS TIME, BEERUS. YOU'RE STILL ALIVE THANKS TO THEM.

PLEASE!!

I REALLY DO, ACTUALLY.

HI!

HERE IT IS.

VMM

ZENÔ-SAMA... THIS TIME...

KAIÔ-SHIN...

ZENÔ-SAMA...

Z... ZE...

PAY YOUR RESPECTS !!!

YOU FOOL!!!!

I WANT YOU TO TAKE US TO HIM NOW.

...!

...

...

HEY, ZEN-CHAN!

AH, GOKU!

JUST AS PROMISED, I BROUGHT YOU A NEW FRIEND.

YES.

LET'S PLAY.

HI.

HI.

WAH!

WAH!

WHIS, WAS THIS **YOUR** IDEA?

NO, IT WAS ALL HIS DOING.

IT ALL WORKED OUT.

HEH HEH HEH ...

I WILL. ONE DAY.

FATHER.

YOU CAN COME VISIT US ANYTIME.

IT MAKES ME ENVIOUS OF UNIVERSE 7.

I SEE.

THANK YOU FOR YOUR HELP. I MUST RETURN TO UNIVERSE 10.

I TRULY APOLOGIZE FOR THE TROUBLE I BROUGHT TO ALL OF YOU.

I UNDERSTAND...

BE CAREFUL WHO YOU ADOPT AS AN APPRENTICE NEXT TIME.

LET'S GO, WHIS.

WELL, THEN.

YES!

SHM

チョコレート Chocolate

THANK YOU, BUT WE'VE MADE OUR DECISION.

HE'S RIGHT.

WHAT? I DON'T KNOW YET... YOU SHOULD JUST STAY HERE WITH US.

...IS IT STILL POSSIBLE FOR US TO GO TO THE TIME BEFORE ZAMAS AND DABRA SHOW UP?

WE ALSO WANT TO GO BACK TO THE FUTURE, BUT...

MOM.

OH, BUT YOU ALSO MADE ANOTHER ONE.

WHIS! DON'T DO ANYTHING STUPID! YOU'RE GOING TO CREATE ANOTHER PARALLEL WORLD!

IS THAT TRUE?!

OF COURSE IT'S POSSIBLE.

HRMM...

...IF ZAMAS SHOWS UP AGAIN, HE MIGHT COME KILL YOU!

YOU CAN'T! I'M NOT SURE ABOUT THIS DABRA GUY, BUT...

HO HO HO. WE HAVE SOMETHING MORE CONVENIENT THAN THE LITTLE JAR THAT YOU BROUGHT WITH YOU.

DON'T YOU DARE UNDER-ESTIMATE THE GOD OF DESTRUC-TION!

WHAT? I SEE...

YOU SHOULD TALK TO THE LORD BEERUS ON THE OTHER SIDE AND HE'LL GIVE YOU A HAND.

IF I MANAGE NOT TO GET KILLED BY DABRA, LORD BEERUS WON'T DIE EITHER.

WHY DIDN'T YOU GUYS TELL ME?!

WHAT...?!

THEN HOW'D YOU DO IT?

NO... I CAN'T KILL IMMOR-TALS...

OH, SO YOU HAVE A TECHNIQUE THAT CAN KILL IMMORTALS?

90

ONLY THIS TIME, I'LL LET IT PASS.

Y-YES...

COME ON...

STOP WHINING. THAT'S PART OF YOUR TRAINING.

TCH...

TRUNKS.

BUT PLEASE REMEMBER, YOU'LL HAVE TO SEE ANOTHER TRUNKS AND MAI LIVING THERE. ARE YOU SURE YOU'RE FINE WITH THAT?

TH-THANK YOU, MY LORD.

FINE. DO AS YOU WISH.

SO, YOU REALLY LEAVING?

YEAH... HAVING TWO OF US WILL DOUBLE THE POWER.

THAT'S FINE.

RIGHT...

MAKE IT COUNT.

LET'S GO, WHIS.

SHM

YEAH.

Super DB

I WILL!

LORD BEERUS.

THANK YOU.

Super DB

WOOSH

ARE YOU SURE YOU WANT TO LEAVE? IF YOU LIKE, I COULD ADOPT YOU AS MY APPRENTICE AND BOTH OF YOU COULD LIVE TOGETHER IN OUR SACRED WORLD.

TAKE THIS CAPSULE SET WITH YOU. THERE'S FOOD AND OTHER NECESSITIES IN IT.

TWO DAYS LATER...

THANK YOU.

1 CAPSULE CORP.

I UNDERSTAND...

I'VE NEVER BEEN IN SUCH A LUXURIOUS POSITION, WHICH IS WHY I'M GOING TO WITHDRAW FROM YOUR APPRENTICESHIP ONCE I DEFEAT BOBIDDI AND DABRA.

I APPRECIATE YOUR OFFER, MY LORD. BUT THE ONLY REASON I BECAME YOUR APPRENTICE WAS TO DESTROY BOBIDDI-- IT WAS ONLY TEMPORARY.

PLEASE SAY HI TO ME ON THE OTHER SIDE.

I WILL.

IT'S HIS WAY OF SETTLING THINGS.

THAT'S NOT THE POINT.

HEY...IF HE QUITS THE APPRENTICESHIP, DOESN'T THAT MEAN HE WON'T BE ABLE TO USE HIS HEALING POWERS ANYMORE? ISN'T THAT A WASTE?

HMMM... I DON'T REALLY GET WHAT'S GOING ON...

94

FAREWELL, EVERYONE!

YOU ARE A MAN OF THE FUTURE. YOU MAY NOT BE ABLE TO REGAIN YOUR LOST TIMELINE, BUT IF THERE'S A CHANCE TO CREATE A WHOLE NEW PEACEFUL ONE, YOU'LL DO IT!

TRUNKS! I'M NOT SMART ENOUGH TO UNDERSTAND DIFFICULT THINGS, BUT I'M SURE YOUR DECISION IS THE RIGHT ONE.

DON'T SLACK OFF ON YOUR TRAINING.

GET STRONGER, TRUNKS.

...

SAY HI TO YOUR MOM ON THE OTHER SIDE!

ANYWAYS, JUST BE HAPPY!

GOKU...

EVERYONE ELSE TOO-- THANK YOU FOR YOUR HELP.

YES, FATHER!

...!

YOU'LL BE JUST FINE WITHOUT US.

GOOD LUCK... TRUNKS!

J-JUST WHAT HAPPENS TO ME IN THE FUTURE?!

DRAGON BALL SUPER

CHAPTER 27: LIFE, TRAINING AND MORE

UNIVERSE 7, EARTH...

...EVERY-ONE'S LIVES CONTINUE PEACE-FULLY...

OBLIVIOUS TO THE INTENSE BATTLE WITH ZAMAS...

THANKS. HAVE A GOOD DAY.

SEE YOU AROUND!

TAP

VwEEEM

VwEEEM

LA DEE DA LA♪ DEE DA♪

AND IN A BACK-WATER TOWN LIKE THIS...

OH? ISN'T THAT THE LATEST AIR TRUCK MODEL?

YEAH...

NEED HELP?

WHAT AN IDIOT!

HMPH! YOU DON'T UNDERSTAND THE SITUATION HERE AT ALL.

...WHEN YOU TRY TO GO AGAINST US.

LET ME TEACH YOU WHAT HAPPENS...

I CAN'T AFFORD TO GIVE IT TO YOU GUYS.

BULMA GAVE ME THIS TRUCK SO I'D WORK HARDER.

WHAT'S SO FUNNY?

HM...?

TAP

SHOOM

TAKE THIS !!!!

104

AH...

I GUESS I'M NOT ONE TO TALK...

GO GET A JOB INSTEAD OF PULLING STUNTS LIKE THIS!

I'LL SHOW YOU...

DIE!!!

BAMBAMBAM

!

FWIP FWIP FWIP FWIP FWIP

HE'S A
MON-
STER
!!!

OH
NO!

GAH!

FLK
FLK

WHAT
SHOULD
I DO?

SHOOT...
HE LEFT HIS
BUDDIES
BEHIND...

BUT I
PROMISED
CHI-CHI THAT
I'D WORK...

I SHOULD
GET BACK TO
TRAINING...

LOOKS
LIKE I'M
GETTING
OUT OF
SHAPE...

HUH?

108

OF COURSE! THESE TWO ARE WANTED CRIMINALS WITH A BOUNTY ON THEIR HEADS!

YOU SURE I CAN HAVE THIS MUCH?

OOOH!

HEY, WHIS!

IT'S THE COMMUNICATION DEVICE I GOT FROM WHIS!

HERE IT IS...

THANKS, MAN!

I'M SURE CHI-CHI WILL LET ME GO BACK TO TRAINING IF I SHOW HER ALL THIS MONEY!

ALL RIGHT!

YOU IN BED? COME ON! I NEED TO GET BACK TO TRAINING.

CAN YOU HEAR ME?

YO?

HE'S NOT RESPONDING...

...

SHHHH

YOUR MOVES ARE GETTING SHARPER.

YOU'RE GETTING BETTER, VEGETA.

I'M BORED.

YAWN!

HRAH!!!

!

BWF

111

112

GRP

CORRECT.

SHUP

I GOT YOU!!!

I DON'T NEED YOUR COMPLIMENTS!

HMPH!

GRAH!

HA!

...

YOU'VE GROWN AS A WARRIOR, VEGETA.

YOU DID WELL.

I'M GOING TO BED.

OKAY, THIS IS ENOUGH.

IT'S A STUPID RIVALRY-- NOT WORTH MY TIME.

AH ...

IT MUST BE BECAUSE SON GOKU WAS STRONGER THAN HIM DURING THE BATTLE WITH ZAMAS.

HE'S MORE INTO THIS THAN USUAL ...

WHAT'S UP WITH HIM?

TUP

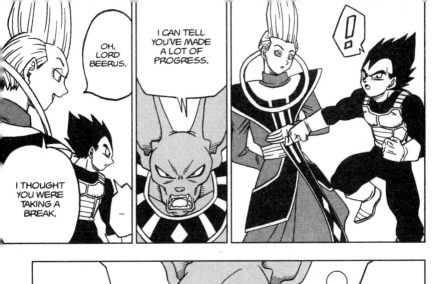

OH, LORD BEERUS.

I CAN TELL YOU'VE MADE A LOT OF PROGRESS.

I THOUGHT YOU WERE TAKING A BREAK.

...

SO...HOW ABOUT WE GO AT IT AGAIN?

I'VE CHANGED MY MIND.

...

YOU SHOULD DO IT, VEGETA.

HOW UNUSUAL.

WHAT?

I AC-CEPT.

VERY WELL...

HRAH!!!!

AH...SO THAT'S WHY.

I'M NOT THE SAME AS I WAS BEFORE...

IT'S BEEN A FEW YEARS...

HWOOSH

YUP. I SAID THOSE TWO SAIYANS WILL BECOME HIS RIVALS ONE DAY.

BY ANY CHANCE, DID YOU SAY SOME-THING TO BEERUS?

SUPER SAIYAN BLUE...

BSH

BWSH

...VEGE-TA.

BRING IT ON...

HOWEVER, YOUR TRANSFORMATION IS JUST A MERE POWER-UP FROM SUPER SAIYAN GOD--THAT'S NOT ENOUGH TO REACH MY LEVEL.

FWP

MY HAND EVEN SHOOK A BIT.

I SEE... THE MOMENT OF IMPACT WAS INDEED MAGNIFICENT.

B AM

GRAH!!!!

TMP

TMP

118

120

KRASH

!!

HMPH...

SPLASH

BURBL
BURBL

HM...? THAT WAS SURPRISINGLY QUICK...

WANNA GO AGAIN?

WHAT'S THIS?

123

PHEW...

SSHH

IF KAKAROT CAN DO IT, SO CAN I!

OOOH?

VEGETA. THAT'S THE SAME FORM GOKU USED! WHEN DID YOU LEARN HOW TO DO THAT?

LET'S CONTINUE!

HEE HEE HEE... THIS IS EXCITING!

124

BUT I WONDER HOW LONG YOU'LL LAST...

YOU'VE IMPROVED A BIT!

GLARE

FWIP

POW POW POW POW POW

SHOOM

BAM BAM BAM BAM BAM

HRAAAAH!!!

TCH...

BUT I BELIEVE IT'S ABOUT TIME HE GOT SERIOUS. IT WOULD BE TROUBLESOME IF HE GOT HIT AND LOST HIS TEMPER...

I DON'T WANT THAT EITHER. HE'S UNPREDICTABLE WHEN HE'S ANGRY...

NO. HE'S STILL PLAYING AROUND.

BAM BAM BAM THOOM

IS BEERUS FIGHTING SERIOUSLY?

I SUPPOSE GOKU IS NO LONGER AHEAD OF HIM.

IT APPEARS VEGETA HAS COMPLETE CONTROL OVER SUPER SAIYAN BLUE.

!

YOU'RE MINE!!!

128

GOT YOU!

...

AH!

OH!

...

HE DID IT!

HE SURE DID.

YOU...

GRP

DON'T GET COCKY.

SKWEEZ

OH?

DID I DROP MY SCEPTER SOME- WHERE...?

WILL DO.

SHF

WHIS! CREATE A BARRIER BEFORE HE GETS OUT OF CONTROL!

HEY!!!

BOO——OM

GOOD-NESS... THAT WAS BIG...

DAM-MIT...

GAH...

YOU GOT CARRIED AWAY WHILE I WAS GOING EASY ON YOU...

AT THIS RATE, IT'LL TAKE YOU A MILLION YEARS TO BECOME MY RIVAL!

TAP

WHIS, FIX THIS MESS.

AS YOU WISH.

YOU COULD PROBABLY BE A CANDIDATE FOR A GOD OF DESTRUC-TION IN ANOTHER UNIVERSE...

WELL...I'LL GIVE YOU POINTS FOR IMPROVING SO QUICKLY.

YOU DID VERY WELL.

YOU DON'T HAVE TO FEEL THE STING OF DEFEAT, VEGETA.

DAMN...

AFTER ALL, YOUR OPPONENT IS THE GOD OF DESTRUCTION OF THIS UNIVERSE.

WHAT DID YOU EXPECT?

I'M NO MATCH FOR HIM AT ALL...

T P

DOING THAT IS LIMITING. IT WILL TAKE SOME TIME FOR YOUR BRAIN AND SENSES TO GET YOUR BODY TO MOVE HOW YOU WANT.

I CAN TELL THAT YOU STILL THINK FIRST AND MOVE LATER.

...THAT'S WHAT YOU'RE SAYING, RIGHT?

ONCE I MASTER IT, I'LL BE ABLE TO TAKE ON ANY ENEMY...

EVEN LORD BEERUS HASN'T MASTERED IT.

YOU MUST BE ABLE TO LET EVERY SINGLE PART OF YOUR BODY JUDGE AND ACT ON ITS OWN.

AND THAT'S VERY DIFFICULT.

INDEED.

KAKAROT AND I ARE EQUALS. BUT WE ARE FAR FROM REACHING OUR FULL POTENTIAL.

?

THAT MEANS... I STILL HAVE A LONG WAY TO GO.

AS LONG AS I KNOW THAT, THAT'S ALL I NEED.

...

I'M SICK OF FOLLOWING AFTER HIM.

I'M THE ONE WHO WILL GET TO THE TOP FIRST.

?

SORRY, BUT I NEED YOU TO TAKE ME BACK TO EARTH.

IS SOMETHING WRONG?

WELL THEN, STARTING TOMORROW, SHALL I INCREASE YOUR TIME FOR TRAINING?

NO. I'LL SAVE THE NEXT SESSION FOR ANOTHER TIME.

SO THAT'S WHAT YOU WERE REFERRING TO.

I SEE.

KLIK KLIK

SOMEONE WAS TRYING TO REACH YOU.

HEEEY, WHIS!

FOR A WHILE?

I WON'T BE COMING BACK HERE FOR QUITE A WHILE.

I WONDER WHO'S CALLING ME.

AH, YES.

I FOUND YOUR SCEPTER.

WHIS, IT'S ME! GOKU!

THERE YOU ARE!

HELLO? WHO ARE YOU??

DAIFUKU?! IT SOUNDS BOLD YET SCRUMPTIOUS.

IT'S REALLY DELICIOUS AND CLASSY!

THAT'S FINE... SO, WHAT ARE YOU BRINGING ME THIS TIME?

IT'S BEEN A WHILE, BUT I WANTED TO ASK YOU TO TRAIN ME AGAIN!

I GOT SOME DAIFUKU FOR YOU!!

HOW CAN I HELP YOU?

OH, GOKU!

CAN WE MEET UP HERE IN AN HOUR?

I'M AT BULMA'S RIGHT NOW. I THOUGHT WE COULD INVITE VEGETA TOO.

BUT VEGETA'S ABOUT TO LEAVE...

WHAT? HOW COME?

HUH?!

THAT'S CHEATING! HE WAS TRAINING WITHOUT ME?! LET ME JOIN YOU GUYS THEN!

OH? VEGETA'S ALREADY HERE WITH ME.

IT'S ALMOST TIME FOR IT TO BE BORN...

...

WHY **ARE** YOU LEAVING, VEGETA?

THANKS FOR COMING TO SEE ME!

SORRY I KEPT YOU WAITING! WELCOME BACK, GOKU!

HUH? A BIRTH?

YOU'RE EATING TOO MUCH!

WHAT'S UP WITH THAT BELLY?

OH BOY...

HA HA HA!

SO HE WAS TALKING ABOUT YOUR BABY, HUH?

HUH? OH, RIGHT. YEAH, YOU DID SAY SOMETHING ABOUT THAT.

I TOLD YOU AREADY-- I'M EXPECTING A SECOND KID!

WHAT?! SO YOU CAME HERE FOR SOMETHING ELSE?

VWEEM

BOOM

ONE HOUR LATER...

NOW, LET'S GET GOING.

THANKS FOR WAITING.

HEY, WHIS!

HOW STUPID ARE YOU?! IF I LEAVE TO GO TRAIN NOW, SHE'LL NEVER FORGIVE ME!

WHY? YOU'RE NOT THE ONE GIVING BIRTH.

CAN'T YOU TELL BY LOOKING AT BULMA? SHE'S GONNA GIVE BIRTH ANY DAY NOW, AND I NEED TO STAY WITH HER.

VEGETA, WHY'RE YOU LEAVING?

LOOK AT ME! I DON'T EVEN KNOW WHEN GOHAN AND GOTEN WERE BORN.

WHY DO YOU CARE?!

138

JUST GO ALREADY!

DON'T BLAME ME IF I GET WAY STRONGER THAN YOU, OKAY?

HUH?

...BUT YOU'RE A HORRIBLE FATHER.

YOU MAY NOT BE A BAD PERSON...

ANYWAY, LET'S GET GOING, SHALL WE?

MAYBE I'M NOT FAMILIAR ENOUGH WITH EARTH CUSTOMS TO UNDERSTAND THIS...

...

I'M DEFINITELY CORRECT HERE... DEFINITELY...

UWOOSH

BY THE WAY, DO YOU HAVE THAT DELICACY CALLED DAIFUKU WITH YOU?

YEAH, OF COURSE!

和
☆☆

EXCELLENT! I LOOK FORWARD TO EATING IT.

139

WHAT'RE YOU TALKING ABOUT?

PROM-ISE?

BEFORE YOU GO, WE SHOULD TALK ABOUT THAT PROMISE WE MADE WITH THE LORD OF EVERY-THING.

WAIT, BEERUS!

...I REALLY AM GONNA TAKE THAT NAP.

NOW THAT I'M FULL...

I'M TALKING ABOUT THE FIGHTING TOURNAMENT ACROSS ALL THE UNIVERSES.

WE DON'T NEED TO DO SOME-THING LIKE THAT!

I WANNA SET A GOAL BEFORE I TRAIN. AT LEAST LET'S MAKE A SCHED-ULE BEFORE YOU GO TO SLEEP!

HEY! BUT IT SOUNDS REALLY EXCITING. IT'S GOING TO DECIDE WHICH UNIVERSE IS REALLY THE STRONGEST!

FORGET THAT NON-SENSE...

I'M NOT JOKING AROUND. DON'T BOTHER THE LORD OF EVERYTHING ANY-MORE.

YOU FOOL!

LOOK! THE LORD OF EVERYTHING GAVE ME THIS SWITCH. I CAN SEE HIM ANYTIME WITH THIS. MAYBE I SHOULD GO ASK HIM.

SHF

YOU FOOL! DON'T GET CARRIED AWAY!

HIM? I DON'T THINK HE'S THAT BAD. LOOK AT HOW ADORABLE HIS FACE IS.

NO! THE LORD OF EVERYTHING HIMSELF IS WHAT'S SCARY.

IS SOMEONE REALLY SCARY GONNA APPEAR??

I'M ONLY ASKING ABOUT THE TOURNAMENT.

WHY?

I WOULDN'T RECOMMEND THAT EITHER. YOU NEVER KNOW WHAT'LL HAPPEN WITH HIM.

ZENŌ-SAMA IS SURELY PURE OF HEART. BUT HIS PURENESS IS WHAT MAKES HIM SO SCARY!

YOU MUST BE VERY CAREFUL...

THIS SIDE BRINGS HIM TO ME...

WHICH ONE SHOULD I CHOOSE?

...AND THIS ONE TAKES ME TO HIM...

FLIP

I AM HIS FRIEND AFTER ALL.

IT'S JUST A TOURNAMENT. IT'LL BE FINE.

DON'T GET COCKY!

PLEASE REMEMBER THAT HE HAS THE POWER TO ANNIHILATE THE ENTIRE UNIVERSE.

142

KLIK

TOO LATE!

I'M TELLING YOU AGAIN-- DON'T PRESS THAT BUTTON!

REALLY, DON'T DO IT!

THIS IS DEFINITELY GONNA BE BAD!!!

THAT IDIOT...

FWIP

GOODNESS... HE REALLY DID IT!

DRAGON BALL SUPER

CHAPTER 28: THE GODS OF DESTRUCTION FROM ALL 12 UNIVERSES

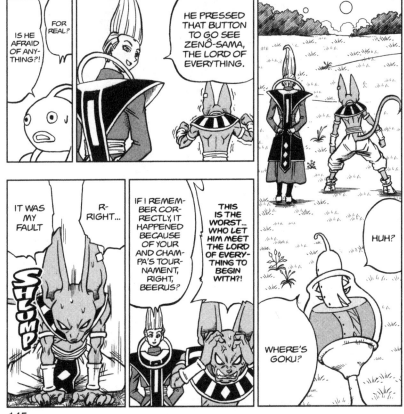

IS HE AFRAID OF ANYTHING?!

FOR REAL?

HE PRESSED THAT BUTTON TO GO SEE ZENŌ-SAMA, THE LORD OF EVERYTHING.

IT WAS MY FAULT

R-RIGHT...

IF I REMEMBER CORRECTLY, IT HAPPENED BECAUSE OF YOUR AND CHAMPA'S TOURNAMENT, RIGHT, BEERUS?

THIS IS THE WORST... WHO LET HIM MEET THE LORD OF EVERYTHING TO BEGIN WITH?!

SHUMP

HUH?

WHERE'S GOKU?

ZENÔ-SAMA'S PALACE

AH.

CHECKMATE, UNIVERSE 7!

...

I ALSO HAVE FIVE MORE.

TAP

BUT I STILL HAVE FIVE MORE TO GO.

HMM...

146

HEY, GRAND PRIEST. HOW ARE THE MORTALS IN THE 12 UNIVERSES DOING LATELY?

IT IS...

ISN'T THIS TOO MANY?

LET'S DO THAT.

WHY DON'T WE GET RID OF A FEW?

THERE HASN'T BEEN MUCH CHANGE WITH THE OTHER UNIVERSES... I WOULD SAY THE OVERALL LEVEL OF THE UNIVERSES MAY HAVE GONE DOWN SLIGHTLY.

UNIVERSE 1 IS IN THE LEAD, AS USUAL. UNIVERSE 12 IS NEXT WITH RECENT, RAPID GROWTH.

WOULD YOU LIKE TO GET RID OF A FEW?

I'M LOSING INTEREST IN OBSERVING THEM ALL.

SO AM I.

IT'S POINTLESS TO KEEP ALL 12 OF THEM.

IT IS.

SO, THEY'RE NOT DEVELOPING UP AT ALL.

THEN LET THE GUIDES IN THE DESIGNATED UNIVERSES WITHDRAW.

VERY WELL, MY LORD.

LET'S ERASE THE EIGHT UNIVERSES THAT ARE LOWER THAN THE OTHERS.

...

YOU'RE RIGHT. I GUESS FOUR IS GOOD ENOUGH.

....!

THAT WAS FAST!

OH, IT'S ZEN-CHAN'S HOUSE!

OH, WE HAVE A GUEST.

MY LORDS, PLEASE HOLD ON A MOMENT.

WHO IS IT?

OH? WHO IS IT?

WHAT'S UP?! ZEN-CHANS.

WHAT DO YOU WANT?

APPARENTLY, HE WANTS TO ASK A FAVOR.

OH, GOKU!

LOOKS LIKE YOU'RE BOTH GETTING ALONG!

I DON'T REMEMBER WHICH ONE OF YOU I PROMISED, BUT WE TALKED ABOUT THE INTERUNIVERSE TOURNAMENT BEFORE, RIGHT?

HOW'S EVERYTHING GOING WITH THAT? I'M TIRED OF WAITING.

YOU'RE RIGHT.

WE CAN'T DO THAT IF WE ERASE THEM.

THAT'S WHAT I THOUGHT.

AH, I FORGOT.

149

FⅬASH

...

IT WILL ONLY TAKE A MOMENT.

FWAP

BUT I GOTTA HURRY!

HUH?

THIS IS THE GRAND PRIEST. DO YOU READ ME?

ALL GUIDE ANGELS.

151

...THE GRAND PRIEST?

THIS IS...

FLK

FLK

NOM

NOM

RSTL

KLNK

AND YOU WENT AND GOT HELP FROM BEERUS?!

SO, IT'S TRUE THAT THAT ZAMAS BASTARD WAS THE ONE WHO DID ALL OF THIS?

LORD RUMS-SHI!

MY DEEP-EST APOLO-GIES...!

I JUST GOT A CALL FROM THE GRAND PRIEST!

OH MY ...

FLK FLK

OF ALL THE GODS OF DE-STRUC-TION, HE IS THE ONE THAT I HATE THE MOST!!

!

WHAT DID YOU SAY?!

EFFECTS ON THE OTHER PLANETS IF THE PLANET'S BEEN DESTROYED... NONE.

POSSIBILITY OF HELPING THEMSELVES ...ZERO PERCENT.

...

FLK FLK

THIS IS THE DUTY OF THE GOD OF DESTRUCTION.

THAT IS NOT POSSIBLE, LORD OF LORDS.

IS THERE REALLY NO OTHER CHANCE FOR THEM TO SURVIVE ...

I REGRET TO SAY THAT THIS PLANET IS SET TO BE DESTROYED.

I'LL CALCULATE THE ODDS AGAIN JUST IN CASE...

...

IF I MAKE ANOTHER MISTAKE, THE GRAND PRIEST WILL GET ANGRY.

I'LL DEAL WITH IT LATER.

I AM WORKING ON A CALCULATION RIGHT NOW.

WE JUST RECEIVED A CALL FROM THE GRAND PRIEST.

LORD SIDRA.

FROM THE GRAND PRIEST ?!

WHAT ?!

MURMUR

HA HA!

OPEN WIDE.

HERE YOU ARE, MY DEAR BELMOD.

WE HAVE ENOUGH TIME. LET'S HAVE FUN UNTIL MORNING.

TODAY IS THE ANNIVERSARY THAT MARKS 87,910,715 DAYS SINCE I BECAME THE GOD OF DESTRUCTION.

OKAY, OKAY.

NO FAIR!

IT'S MY TURN.

GULP

NOM NOM

YUP! THIS IS GOOD!

LORD BELMOD. THERE'S SOMETHING I NEED TO TELL YOU.

!

THIS IS...

FLK FLK FLK

YEAH!

HA HA!

DO YOU WANNA DIE?!

HOW DARE YOU BARGE IN LIKE THIS!

WHAT'S YOUR PROBLEM?!

AH...

AGH...

POOR THING... SHE WAS JUST AN INNOCENT GIRL.

HMPH... I WAS GOING TO DESTROY THIS PLANET ANYWAY.

VERY MUCH SO.

WE ARE.

ARE WE IN A RUSH?

ANYWAY, WHAT'S WRONG, MARCARITA?

EEEEK!!!!

E...

I ASSUME YOU ARE ALL LISTENING.

IS EVERYONE READY?

THERE IS SOMETHING I NEED TO TELL YOU. I WANT ALL OF YOUR GODS OF DESTRUCTION AS WELL AS YOUR LORDS OF LORDS TO REPORT TO THE PALACE.

THAT'S ALL.

WILL THEY REALLY ALL COME OVER HERE JUST LIKE THAT?

HUH...?

LET'S WAIT A MINUTE.

THEY WILL.

THIS IS AMAZING!!!

THESE ARE THE GODS OF ALL THE UNIVERSES!!!

AN EMERGENCY CALL... HOW LONG HAS IT BEEN SINCE THE LAST ONE?

...

LET US WAIT FOR THE ARRIVAL OF THOSE FROM UNIVERSE 8.

PLEASE RISE, LADIES AND GENTLEMEN.

ROH
UNIVERSE 9
LORD OF LORDS

SIDRA
UNIVERSE 9
GOD OF DESTRUCTION

MOHITO
UNIVERSE 9
GUIDE ANGEL

164

YOU'RE ALWAYS MAKING A MESS FOR THE REST OF US!

THAY GUY MUST'VE DONE SOMETHING AGAIN...!!

FUWA
UNIVERSE 6
LORD OF LORDS

CHAMPA
UNIVERSE 6
GOD OF
DESTRUCTION

VADOS
UNIVERSE 6
GUIDE ANGEL

BEERUS DID SOMETHING AGAIN...!

TCH...

KURU
UNIVERSE 4
LORD OF LORDS

QUITELA
UNIVERSE 4
GOD OF
DESTRUCTION

CONIC
UNIVERSE 4
GUIDE ANGEL

MAY I ASK YOU ABOUT THE GENTLEMAN BEHIND YOU?

MY LORD.

THIS MAN, MY LORD, IS TOPPO.

LORD BELMOD.

OH.

I AM TOPPO, AT YOUR SERVICE.

TO TELL YOU THE TRUTH, I AM PLANNING ON RETIRING ANY DAY NOW. I AM TRAINING HIM TO SUCCEED ME AS THE NEXT GOD OF DESTRUCTION. BECAUSE HE HAPPENED TO BE WITH ME, I BROUGHT HIM ALONG FOR THE EXPERIENCE.

PLEASE WORK HARD TO BECOME A GREAT GOD OF DESTRUCTION.

UNDERSTOOD.

M-MY SINCERE THANKS TO YOU FOR SUCH KIND WORDS.

TOPPO
UNIVERSE 11
CANDIDATE FOR GOD OF DESTRUCTION

KAI
UNIVERSE 11
LORD OF LORDS

BELMOD
UNIVERSE 11
GOD OF DESTRUCTION

MARCARITA
UNIVERSE 11
GUIDE ANGEL

NOW THEN... PLEASE COME.

SST

WE ARE READY NOW.

MY LORD, GRAND PRIEST.

HA HA HA!!

ILLE
UNIVERSE 8
LORD OF LORDS

LIQUIIR
UNIVERSE 8
GOD OF
DESTRUCTION

KORUN
UNIVERSE 8
GUIDE ANGEL

MY...MY APOLOGIES FOR KEEPING YOU WAITING!!

GULP

GULP

WELL THEN, THE LORD OF EVERYTHING HAS AN ANNOUNCEMENT.

EVERYONE'S NOW HERE.

HUH? TOURNAMENT OF POWER?

...WE HAVE DECIDED TO HOLD THE **TOURNAMENT OF POWER**— A TOURNAMENT IN WHICH THE CHOSEN FIGHTERS FROM EACH UNIVERSE WILL COMPETE.

I AM FULLY AWARE THAT THIS IS SUDDEN, BUT IN FIVE TIKS, PRECISELY AT 157 O'CLOCK, DAY 3,135,500,603 OF THE KING CALENDAR...

AGU
UNIVERSE 12
LORD OF LORDS

GEENE
UNIVERSE 12
GOD OF DESTRUCTION

MARTINNE
UNIVERSE 12
GUIDE ANGEL

CHOSEN FIGHTERS... WHAT DO YOU MEAN...?

OGMA
UNIVERSE 5
LORD OF LORDS

ARACK
UNIVERSE 5
GOD OF DESTRUCTION

CUCATAIL
UNIVERSE 5
GUIDE ANGEL

BEEP!

BEEP!

LORD MOSCO! YOU MUST NEVER SAY SUCH THINGS IN ZENÔ-SAMA'S PRESENCE!

...THAT IDIOT MADE ZENÔ-SAMA'S PLAN A REALITY...

JUST AS I THOUGHT...

HE REALLY DID IT...

LORD OF LORDS FROM UNIVERSE 3.

ARE YOU HAVING TROUBLE THERE?

WHAT?

IT'S NOTHING, MY LORD!!

UM, NO!

SWF

WHAT DID HE JUST SAY?

EYRE
UNIVERSE 3
LORD OF LORDS

MOSCO
UNIVERSE 3
GOD OF DESTRUCTION

KAMPARI
UNIVERSE 3
GUIDE ANGEL

IS THAT BAD?

HUH?

LORD MOSCO WAS SIMPLY CONCERNED THAT WE HAVE SO LITTLE TIME TO PREPARE...

A-AS IT IS...

EVERY-THING IS ALL RIGHT, MY LORD.

AH! UH... NO!!

I KNEW THEY'D WANT IT TO BE AS SOON AS POSSIBLE!!

I KNEW IT.

LORD MOSCO NOW SAYS IT IS OUTSTANDING THAT WE CAN PARTICIPATE SO QUICKLY.

MUR MUR

HA HA HA...

AH...

IT'S SOMETIMES NECESSARY TO STRETCH THE TRUTH, MY DEAR LORD OF LORDS.

THAT WAS A CLOSE ONE...

YES.

AH, YOU MEAN THE TOURNAMENT OF POWER.

WHAT?

HE SAYS HE DOESN'T UNDERSTAND WHAT'S GOING ON.

IS SOMETHING WRONG?

INDEED, ZEN8-SAMA, WHO CAME FROM THE FUTURE, HAS NEVER SEEN ONE BEFORE.

I SEE.

ALLOW ME TO SET UP A TOURNAMENT STAGE!

パチン

LET US INITIATE A QUICK **ZEN** EXHIBITION MATCH, SHALL WE?

WELL THEN...

ALL RIGHT!

OH!

YOU MEAN RIGHT HERE?

HUH? RIGHT NOW?

OH!

FWP

IT'S A STAGE ...!

TH...

THIS IS...

PLEASE ENTER THE STAGE.

NOW THEN, MY DEAR GODS OF DESTRUCTION.

I GOT THROWN OVER HERE TOO!

YOU BASTARD. HOW MANY TIMES HAVE I TOLD YOU TO BE CAREFUL...

GOKU!!

WHAT?!!

HOLD ON A MOMENT. THIS TOURNAMENT OF POWER REQUIRES THE GODS OF DESTRUCTION TO PARTICIPATE AS WELL?

US...?! WHAT DO YOU MEAN...?!

GOWAS
UNIVERSE 10
LORD OF LORDS

RUMSSHI
UNIVERSE 10
GOD OF
DESTRUCTION

KUSU
UNIVERSE 10
GUIDE ANGEL

HOW SURPRISING FOR US GODS OF DESTRUCTION TO FIGHT EACH OTHER.

WOW, IS THIS FOR REAL?!!!

IT IS ONLY NATURAL THAT YOU WOULD BE REPRESENTATIVES IN THIS BATTLE.

YOU ARE EACH FROM DIFFERENT UNIVERSES...

ANATO
UNIVERSE 1
LORD OF LORDS

IWNE
UNIVERSE 1
GOD OF DESTRUCTION

AWAMO
UNIVERSE 1
GUIDE ANGEL

HURRY UP.

THIS IS BAD. I HAVEN'T TRAINED IN DECADES...

THIS IS GETTING OUT OF HAND...

RIGHT AWAY!!!

YES, MY LORD!!!

YES, YOU'VE BEEN AVOIDING IT.

THUD

TAP
TAP

...SHALL BE TERMINATED, ACCORDING TO HIS MAJESTY.

THOSE WHO REFUSE TO GIVE IT THEIR ALL, BY THE WAY...

WHAT ARE THE RULES OF THIS FIGHT?

MY LORD, GRAND PRIEST...

HE IS ALSO OFFERING A REWARD FOR THOSE WHO LAST UNTIL THE VERY END.

ZENÔ-SAMA WANTS TO PLAN OUT THE REST AFTER OBSERVING THIS BATTLE ROYALE.

HERE IT COMES...! THIS IS WHAT'S REALLY SCARY ABOUT ZENÔ-SAMA...

OH WELL. I GUESS IT COULD BE A GOOD OPPORTUNITY TO DECIDE WHO'S THE STRONGEST GOD OF DESTRUCTION, RIGHT, BEERUS?

I GOT IT...

THIS IS MADNESS!

HAVING THEM ALL FIGHT EACH OTHER AT ONCE...

QUITELA.

YOU'RE ALWAYS PICKING A FIGHT WITH ME, HUH?

I CAN'T LET MYSELF BE DESTROYED IN A PLACE LIKE THIS...

WHO DO YOU THINK IS RESPONSIBLE FOR ALL THIS?!!!

GOKU!!!!

QUIT BEING SUCH AN IDIOT!!!

I'M NOT GONNA LOSE IN HAND-TO-HAND COMBAT!!

I LOST TO YOU AT ARM WRESTLING!!!

YOU LOST TO ME ONCE. WHY WILL YOU NEVER ACCEPT THAT I AM STRONGER?

URK

GOOD LUCK, BEERUS!

UGH...

SO IT'S BECAUSE OF BEERUS'S UNIVERSE...

OH GOODNESS, UNIVERSE 7 IS AT IT AGAIN.

IS HE THE REASON FOR ALL OF THIS?

THAT IS...A MORTAL FROM UNIVERSE 7?

WELL, US GODS OF DESTRUCTION ALL HOLD A GRUDGE AGAINST YOU ANYWAY.

HEE HEE... YOU JUST DUG YOUR OWN GRAVE. NOW WE ALL KNOW WHO TO BEAT THE CRAP OUT OF FIRST.

CRAP...!

IF I REMEMBER CORRECTLY, IN THE LAST EMERGENCY CALL, EVERY UNIVERSE WAS ON THE VERGE OF BEING ERASED, THANKS TO YOU.

DON'T TELL US YOU FORGOT ABOUT IT, MY FRIEND.

...

LONG AGO, WE HELD AN ALL-UNIVERSES INVITATIONAL HIDE-AND-SEEK-TOURNAMENT. IT WAS ZENÔ-SAMA'S IDEA.

IT GOES BACK TO BEFORE YOU BECAME THE LORD OF LORDS.

HUH?! HIDE-AND-SEEK?!

WHAT HAPPENED BEFORE?

THE TOURNAMENT HAD TO BE CANCELED SINCE HE NEVER CAME OUT. HIS MAJESTY, WHO WAS TRULY ENJOYING THE EVENT, BECAME FURIOUS. IN ORDER TO CALM HIS ANGER, THE REST OF THE GODS FROM THE 11 OTHER UNIVERSES HAD TO MAKE EXTREMELY INTENSIVE EFFORTS TO PLEASE HIM. DUE TO THAT, THEY ALL HAVE ANIMOSITY TOWARD LORD BEERUS.

FOR THAT TOURNAMENT, LORD BEERUS WENT TO HIDE AND THEN FELL ASLEEP FOR OVER 50 YEARS.

HE'S A TROUBLE-MAKER.

WHAT... HOW COULD HE...

WELL, ASIDE FROM THAT, THERE AP-PEAR TO BE SOME PERSONAL GRUDGES TOO.

178

WHIS, WHAT'S GOING ON?

HE DODGED THEM ALL!!

HIS BODY CAN SENSE ATTACKS AND CAN MAKE DECISIONS TO DODGE THEM.

WHAT'S GOING ON?! IT'S LIKE BEERUS HAS EYES IN THE BACK OF HIS HEAD!

GR !
P

EVEN LORD BEERUS ISN'T PERFECT...

AH! THEY CAUGHT HIM.

GAH!!!

SHF

SHF

ARE THEY ALL STILL ALIVE AFTER THAT?

MAN... BEERUS ISN'T HOLDING BACK.

...

...

I SUPPOSE THEY ARE.

BOOM!

HA HA. NO ONE CAN MATCH MY SPEED WHEN IT COMES TO BARRIERS...

SIDRA... YOU SAVED US ALL.

SHF

PHEW...

THEY HID BEHIND A BARRIER.

THOOM

SIDRA!!!

UGH!!!

ONLY ONE OF US CAN BE AT THE TOP. YOU SHOULD KNOW WE DON'T HAVE THE LUXURY OF HELPING EACH OTHER.

IT'S NOT LIKE BEERUS IS THE ONLY ENEMY HERE, RIGHT?

BEL-MOD... YOU JERK!

I SAW TOO MANY OPEN-INGS TO HOLD BACK.

MY BAD.

HA HA HA! THIS IS GREAT!!

...

THE HELL WITH THAT EXCITING CRAP, STUPID RAT!!

IT'S GETTING MORE AND MORE EXCITING.

I'M GETTING MORE AND MORE EXCITED!

YES! I CAN'T WAIT.

KEEP WATCHING. THIS WILL DEFINITELY BE FUN TO SEE.

NOW... THIS IS WHERE THE REAL MATCH BEGINS.

IS IT GOING TO BE CRAZIER THAN THIS?!

WELL, WELL... LET US SEE HOW IT GOES...

TO BE CONTINUED!

YOU REALLY DON'T MIND ME LIVING HERE TOO?

THANKS.

THERE ARE PLENTY OF ROOMS HERE, SO PICK WHICHEVER ONE YOU LIKE.

A FEW DAYS AFTER BATTLING ZAMAS... HAVING LOST A FUTURE TO RETURN TO, TRUNKS IS PREPARING TO LIVE IN THE PRESENT...

BONUS STORY

THAT YOU, TRUNKS?!

COOL. NOW WE CAN HANG OUT FOREVER.

THANK YOU SO MUCH.

I'VE ONLY EVER HAD MY TRUNKS WITH ME, SO IT'LL BE GREAT HAVING YOU AROUND, KIND OF LIKE A DAUGHTER.

NOT AT ALL! YOU'RE MORE THAN WELCOME, IN FACT.

WHY DIDN'T ANYONE TELL ME?

OH BOY, IT REALLY IS YOU!

THAT MAKES SENSE.

WELL, I ACTUALLY STARTED TRAINING IN THE GRAVITY CHAMBER A LITTLE WHILE AGO. YOU SEE, THESE DAYS, NOBODY GIVES ME A CALL WHEN IT'S TIME TO FIGHT... FIGURED I SHOULD KEEP FROM GETTING RUSTY, JUST IN CASE.

G-GOHAN! WHY'RE YOU HERE?

THOUGH IT'S ALWAYS SO PEACEFUL AROUND HERE, SO MAYBE NO NEED? HA HA HA...

IT'S GOHAN ALL GROWN UP! HE LOOKS JUST LIKE MY GOHAN, FROM THE FUTURE... LIKE HE'S BACK FROM THE DEAD.

...

HEY, GOHAN?

...

TRUTH IS...

SO HOW LONG'RE YOU STAYING HERE?

...THAT I SAVED...

TH-THE PEACEFUL FUTURE...

I'D LOVE TO VISIT SOMETIME, NOW THAT YOU'VE SAVED THE FUTURE AND ALL...

GUESS YOUR FUTURE WORLD'S ALSO PRETTY PEACEFUL WITH YOU AROUND, RIGHT?

REALLY? LOOKING FORWARD IT!

...BUT ONE OF THESE DAYS, YEAH? I'LL SHOW YOU HOW PEACEFUL IT REALLY IS.

I'M AFRAID I CAN'T INVITE YOU TO THE FUTURE RIGHT NOW...

SO SOON? WISH YOU COULD STICK AROUND.

...WE'RE PROBABLY HEADING BACK IN TWO OR THREE DAYS.

THE TRUTH IS...

HUH?

JOLT!

CAN'T WAIT TO MEET YOUR VERSION OF BULMA.

THAT WAS HOW TRUNKS DECIDED TO RETURN TO HIS PEACEFUL FUTURE, BEFORE ZAMAS EVER APPEARED...

MAI... CHANGE OF PLANS. LET'S GO BACK TO THE FUTURE, BEFORE IT WAS DESTROYED...

S-SURE.

WHY? HOW SO?

YOU'RE AS INSENSITIVE AS YOUR FATHER, SOMETIMES.

(APPEARED IN THE JUMP VICTORY CARNIVAL OFFICIAL 2017 GUIDEBOOK)

YOU'RE READING
THE WRONG WAY!

Dragon Ball Super reads from right to left, starting in the
upper-right corner. Japanese is read from right to left,
meaning that action, sound effects, and word-balloon
order are completely reversed from English order.